Deschutes

P9-AGU-554

Desert Hiking Tips

Desert Hiking Tips

EXPERT ADVICE ON
DESERT HIKING AND DRIVING

Second Edition

Bruce Grubbs

FALCONGUIDES

GUILFORD, CONNECTICUT

FALCONGUIDES®

An imprint of The Rowman & Littlefield Publishing Group, Inc.
4501 Forbes Blvd., Ste. 200
Lanham, MD 20706
www.rowman.com
Falcon and FalconGuides are registered trademarks and Make Adventure Your Story is a trademark of The Rowman & Littlefield Publishing Group, Inc.

Distributed by NATIONAL BOOK NETWORK

Copyright © 2020 The Rowman & Littlefield Publishing Group, Inc.

Illustrations by Bruce Grubbs

British Library Cataloguing in Publication Information available

Library of Congress Cataloging-in-Publication Data available

ISBN 978-1-4930-4972-1 (paper)
ISBN 978-1-4930-4973-8 (electronic)

Contents

Acknowledgments

During more than 30 years of desert hiking, many people have shared their ideas and techniques with me. Most will have to remain unnamed, but I want to single out a few. At the top of the list is Bill Sewrey, who was a mentor and an inspiration to an entire generation of Arizona hikers. I especially wish to thank Jean Rukkila for an excellent job of proofreading and for her many suggestions and tips. Many thanks to Russ Schneider, my editor on the first edition, and John Burbidge and Emily Chiarelli, my editors on the second edition, for working with me to make the second edition into a better book. And thanks to all the fine folks at Falcon Publishing. And finally, heartfelt thanks to Duart Martin for encouraging and supporting this project every step of the way.

Introduction

This book covers desert hiking, the art of foot travel in arid country. Although many of the techniques and much of the equipment covered here may be useful for hikers in other desert regions of the world, this advice is aimed squarely at backcountry travel in the deserts of the American Southwest.

CHARACTER OF DESERT BACKCOUNTRY

The desert Southwest includes most of Arizona, New Mexico, Utah, and Nevada, as well as portions of Colorado, California, Oregon, and Idaho, and includes four deserts—the Great Basin, Mohave, Sonoran, and Chihuahuan. Each of these four deserts has different precipitation patterns and habitats. A desert is usually defined as a region that receives less than a specified amount of annual precipitation, for example, 12 inches per year, but there is no agreement on this number. Another technical definition is that plant and animal life is sparse in a desert due to the difficulty of survival under extreme conditions. And that leads to a practical definition—for the backcountry traveler, a desert is simply a place where the availability of water dominates trip planning and the hike itself. Because of heat and dehydration, day hikers must make water the heaviest part of their load.

Hiking is a strenuous activity, and you'll need to drink from 1 to 2 gallons a day to stay hydrated. Failure to bring enough water is the most common cause of rescues of day hikers in the desert. Because water weighs 8.3 pounds per gallon, it's not practical for backpackers on multiday trips to carry more than two days' water supply. So the entire route and campsites must be planned around available water sources.

Even in areas where water is plentiful, such as the Sierra Nevada, desert techniques such as dry camping can enable you to avoid heavily used campsites and their attendant problems: rodent and bear attacks on your food supply. In addition, deserts can be divided into cold and hot—the Sonoran Desert of southern Arizona and northwestern Mexico is a classic hot desert, while the Great Basin Desert of northern Nevada is a cold desert. Sometimes the term *cold desert* is used to refer to extremely cold areas, such as the Arctic and Antarctic regions, where precipitation is also extremely low, but travel in those areas is outside the scope of this book.

Hot Deserts

The Mohave, covering western Arizona, southeast California, and the southern tip of Nevada, is the hottest and driest of the American deserts. Most precipitation falls as gentle winter rain, and some parts of the desert receive no moisture at all in a typical year. Winter temperatures are mild, rarely dipping much below freezing, but summers are very hot, exceeding 120°F in the lowest-elevation areas.

The Chihuahuan Desert covers southern New Mexico, western Texas, a bit of southeastern Arizona, and northeastern Mexico, and also has only one wet season—the summer. Moist air moving off the Gulf of Mexico triggers numerous afternoon thunderstorms, but winter precipitation is rare. Temperatures range from 105°F to around 25°F.

Covering northwestern Mexico, southern Arizona, and a bit of southeastern California, the Sonoran Desert is unique among the American deserts in that it has two rainy seasons—late summer, when the same North American monsoon that brings rains to the Chihuahuan Desert brings summer thunderstorms to the Sonoran, and winter, when storm fronts moving off the Pacific Ocean bring more gentle and prolonged rains to the desert. Temperatures range from 120°F down to around 25°F. Snow does fall occasionally in the winter in the highest parts of the desert but melts quickly.

In the hot deserts, summer is not the best season for hiking—at the lowest elevations, even early mornings are uncomfortably warm. Fall and spring are the best seasons, and even the winters are mild, with daytime temperatures in the 60s or 70s and nights that rarely fall to freezing.

Cold Deserts

The Great Basin Desert, covering most of Nevada, western Utah, and far northern Arizona, is a cold desert. It usually sees some snowfall during the winter months, and the summer heat is not as extreme. Winter temperatures can be subzero at the highest elevations, and the lower valleys can reach 100°F during the summer. Spring and fall are the best hiking seasons, though both summer and winter are enjoyable if you are properly prepared.

1

Gear for Desert Hiking

The equipment for desert hiking differs somewhat from that needed for trips in well-watered country. This chapter presents a few suggestions; there's more information in the following chapters on technique. You can use the following gear checklist as a reminder of items to take, both in your pack and your vehicle, though you won't need every item on every trip. There's more information on specific items after the checklist.

CHECKLIST

☐ water

☐ sun hat

☐ sunscreen

☐ sunglasses

☐ extra clothing

☐ lighter (fire starting)

☐ knife

- ☐ LED headlamp or flashlight
- ☐ extra food
- ☐ map
- ☐ compass
- ☐ first-aid and repair kit
- ☐ insect repellent
- ☐ water filter system
- ☐ purification tablets
- ☐ plastic water bottles
- ☐ collapsible containers
- ☐ lightweight boots
- ☐ socks
- ☐ water shoes
- ☐ walking stick or trekking poles
- ☐ long-sleeved shirt
- ☐ long pants or convertible pants
- ☐ shorts
- ☐ down or fleece jacket
- ☐ rain gear
- ☐ lightweight synthetic underwear

☐ food

☐ cooking gear

☐ day pack or fanny pack

☐ multiday pack

☐ rain cover

☐ tarp or net tent

☐ groundsheet

☐ foam sleeping pad

☐ sleeping bag

Vehicle Supplies

☐ spare tire

☐ lug wrench

☐ jack

☐ jumper cables

☐ extra oil

☐ extra drinking/radiator water

☐ sand mats (old pieces of carpet)

☐ tow rope or chain

KEY EQUIPMENT

Water is always the most important and heaviest single item in your pack. A **sun hat** with an effective brim is essential for keeping your head cool and avoiding heat-related health problems. A pair of good **sunglasses** is nearly essential in the intense desert light of spring and summer.

The hot desert sun will burn your skin quickly, even if you already have a tan. Use a **sun lotion** with a sun protection factor (SPF) of at least 15; SPF 30 is better. Very high SPFs are a waste of money. According to dermatologists, mineral-based sunscreens are best—these contain titanium and zinc oxides, which physically block the sun's damaging rays. Look for micro-fine sunscreens—these rub into the skin more effectively than older formulas, and don't leave a white residue on your skin.

You might be surprised to learn that cold can be a problem in the desert. After dark, temperatures fall rapidly, even in summer, because of the clear, dry air. Since the best seasons for desert hiking are fall, winter, and spring, cold can be even more of a factor. Bring an **extra layer of clothing**, such as a fleece jacket or a shell. Always carry some means of **starting a fire.**

TIP

Disposable cigarette lighters are very light and provide a sustained flame, which helps starting a fire when tinder and wood are damp. I prefer to bring at least two along.

A **knife** is essential for preparing kindling from wet desert wood in an emergency and has many other uses as well. A "Swiss Army Knife" or small multi-tool containing small scissors as well as other tools is the most useful.

Carry an **LED headlamp** or flashlight for use around camp and for hiking in the dark if you are delayed.

LED lights never burn out and their batteries last much longer than incandescent lights. The best batteries are AAA- or AA-size disposable lithium. Lithium batteries work better in temperature extremes and are lighter than other batteries. If your headlamp uses rechargeable batteries, make sure you can replace them in the field, either with a charged battery, or fresh disposable batteries.

Always have some **extra food** along, such as energy bars, even on the shortest hikes, in case you're delayed or decide to extend the hike. You should carry a good **printed map** of your planned hiking area.

Always have a **compass** along. Buy a good-quality, liquid-filled compass. You don't need a fancy model with sighting mirrors and all the extra features for general desert travel, unless you will be triangulating. Always get a compass that is reliable. Your compass may languish in the bottom of your pack for years, but when you do need it, you'll need it badly.

You may find a GPS receiver or a phone with a backcountry mapping app to be useful, but don't use them without a paper map and a compass. All electronic devices can fail, and the batteries will eventually die.

Carry a **first-aid and repair kit** appropriate to the length of the trip and the number of people in the hiking party—and know how to use it.

Buy a first-aid kit specific to the outdoors and the size of your party.

Include a good signal mirror in your first-aid kit. In sunny weather, a mirror flash can easily be seen dozens of miles away and lets searchers pinpoint your location.

Get a signal mirror with a sighting grid, which makes the mirror more accurate and easier to use. Glass mirrors produce a far brighter flash than metal or plastic mirrors, but a small glass mirror works as well as a large one.

Avoid cheap sunglasses. Most are made of plastic and don't protect your eyes from damaging ultraviolet light. In fact, they can be worse than no sunglasses at all. Your pupils open up in response to the decreased visible light and admit more ultraviolet light than they would without sunglasses. The manufacturers of good sunglasses not only make optically correct lenses but also specify the amount of ultraviolet, infrared, and visible light transmitted.

WATER

Water is always the most important and heaviest single item in your pack. Desert hiking centers on water—a person doing strenuous hiking in hot weather may need as much as 2 gallons per day to avoid dehydration. And water is heavy—8.3 pounds per gallon. The availability of water sources usually controls your trip itinerary. On day hikes you can carry all the water you need, although it can still be quite a load in hot weather.

On day hikes, make sure you know where springs, creeks, and other water sources are located, in case you run out of water, or someone gets injured.

When backpacking, carefully plan your trip so you pass at least one reliable water source per day. Sources include permanent or seasonal streams, springs, water pockets or tanks, and water caches placed in advance. It can be difficult to determine whether a water source is in fact reliable, but it's critical that you do, especially in hot weather. Consult hikers experienced in the area, guidebooks, and the land-management agencies for information. As you gain experience yourself, you will be able to predict if seasonal water sources will be available, based on recent weather.

Don't rely on maps for water source information. Even the maps in the otherwise excellent US Geological Survey topographic series often show springs that have long been dry, and are notorious for showing permanent desert streams where, in reality, water flows only during wet weather.

Always have a backup plan in case a critical water source is dry. For example, you should always make certain that you have enough water to backtrack to the last source, or to change your route to one with more water.

A massive load of water can slow you down enough to force a change in your trip plans. Keep this in mind when planning your trip at home, and also during the trip. If a water source is unexpectedly dry, you may have to carry more water than your planning indicated.

Minimizing Your Impact on Desert Water

Because desert water is scarce, all of us must work extra hard to keep it unpolluted. Keep human waste, soap, and food scraps out of drainages, whether or not they are dry at the moment. Never bathe or swim in a water pocket or tank. Even if you don't use soap, you'll still disturb the natural environment by stirring up sand and sediment. Some animals, such as the spadefoot toad, depend on the sediments for successful reproduction.

If water sources are small, take only the water you need for drinking and cooking. And don't waste it. If water is really scarce, even brushing your teeth should be avoided. Remember, you're the guest in the desert backcountry—don't deprive wildlife of water they need to survive.

If water is plentiful and you feel the need to clean up, carry water well away from the source and all drainages, both dry and wet, and give yourself a sponge bath. Use biodegradable soap or shampoo, and use it as sparingly as possible.

Carrying Water

On day hikes in cool weather, you may only need to carry a quart or two per person. One-quart plastic water bottles do the job nicely in this case. Buy bottles made of high-density polyethylene, polycarbonate, polypropylene, or another plastic that doesn't flavor the water. Avoid metal—it quickly becomes hot. Insulated metal water bottles work but are heavy.

In hot weather you might have to carry a gallon or two, even on day hikes. Many extended desert backpacking trips are only possible if you're willing to carry water for a couple of days of dry hiking. Rigid plastic bottles are too bulky, so collapsible water bottles are the answer. They take up almost no room in your pack when empty, and have become as reliable as rigid bottles.

I prefer laminated bottles, which are now made by several companies. These bottles are constructed from laminated plastic, and though the plastic seems stiff, it is remarkably durable. Available in various sizes, they are much lighter than rigid bottles.

Collapsible bottles make it easy to avoid overused campsites near water sources. Just pick up enough water for camp and then hike on for a bit. If you know how to dry camp, you can camp in some fine places, such as ridgetops or even mountaintops.

TIP

Gallon jugs of drinking water from a supermarket are a good way to carry extra water in your vehicle. But don't use them for water caches or any place where they are exposed to the sun—the plastic rots in the sun and becomes brittle.

TIP

Duct tape will temporarily repair most water bottles and collapsible containers.

Even when camped near water, collapsible containers save making multiple trips for water. Carry a couple of spare caps for collapsible bottles. Test all water bottles before a trip by inverting filled bottles and squeezing them hard.

In warm weather, when your water supply is critical, it's a good idea to carry several smaller containers, rather than one or two large containers. I carry a mix of 1-liter bottles for convenient drinking during the day, and for backpacking, I'll add several bottles with 2-liter capacity. When my water supply is critical, I never depend on a single bottle of any type.

If you'll be collecting water from shallow rain pockets, bring along a small bottle or shallow cup with a thin rim. Some people carry large plastic syringes for this purpose.

If the weather's warm, keep most of your water containers inside your pack, insulated by clothing. Bottles carried on your belt or a fanny pack quickly become tepid or worse. Metal canteens are less than desirable because they heat up rapidly. There's nothing less refreshing than a drink of hot water on a hot day.

The ability to find water in an emergency is a valuable skill. Look for patches of lighter-green vegetation in drainages or on distant slopes, which can mark springs. Water pockets often form where floodwaters in otherwise dry washes flow over exposed bedrock. Plunge pools may hold water at the base of dry falls. Damp areas in otherwise dry streambeds are an indication that water is near the surface. Before you start to dig for it, check around the corner. Chances are the water will surface either upstream or downstream. In basin and range country, streams may flow down out of the mountains and disappear abruptly when the stream crosses the fault line at the foot of the range. Rain pockets can sometimes be found where there are large expanses of open, flat, or domed rock. Sandstone country is especially good for rain pockets. Larger pockets can hold water for weeks after a storm. As you gain experience in the desert, you'll automatically take note of signs of water as you travel.

Purifying Water

All wilderness water sources should be purified before use. Even sparkling clear water may contain dangerous organisms. There are several reliable methods for purifying water, including filtration, boiling, and chemical treatment. Filters are popular because they preserve the taste of the water, but most do not remove viruses, which are so small that they pass right through filters. They are also heavy, slow, and tend to clog up, especially in murky water. Check that your filter is easily cleaned in the field before relying on it.

Boiling is a reliable purification method; all you must do is bring water to a rolling boil to kill all disease organisms. This works at any altitude because the boiling point is always high enough to sterilize the water. The disadvantage is that boiling takes time and fuel, and the water tastes flat afterward.

You can improve the taste of boiled water by pouring it back and forth between two containers several times, which aerates the water and helps it cool.

Iodine water purification tablets are also very reliable for purifying water, if used correctly, and they work quickly. Follow the directions on the bottle and keep the tablets dry. Some people find the iodine taste objectionable. It can be removed with the iodine remover tablets that come with some brands of iodine tablets. You can also use fruit or sports drink mixes to hide the taste. Both methods use ascorbic acid (vitamin C), which deactivates the iodine in the water. Be sure you've allowed enough time for the iodine to work before adding either the remover tablets or drink mix to the water. Chlorine dioxide tablets are the most effective water purification method, but they are expensive and time-consuming to use.

A lightweight water filter works well for purifying
water in the desert backcountry.

Desert water is often standing water and contains bits of leaves and other organic material. A lightweight filter system can be made from paper coffee filters and a plastic filter holder. Don't try to use coffee filters without the holder—they work very slowly without the support of the holder. Iodine or chlorine dioxide tablets, coffee filters, and the filter holder make up a water purification system that can handle any desert water source, and still weighs much less than a regular water filter.

FOOTWEAR

After proper fit, ventilation is the important feature to look for in desert hiking boots. Waterproof boots are seldom necessary, except possibly during rainy periods in winter. Avoid heavy, full-grain leather boots. If you insist on waterproof boots, consider a model made with one of the lightweight waterproof/breathable fabrics such as GORE-TEX. Many of the current lightweight boot designs work well in the desert. Desert trails tend to be rocky and abrasive, so look for a boot with leather toe and heel caps, as well as reinforced stitching. Many desert hikers prefer low-cut trail-running shoes or cross-trainers instead of boots.

Strangely enough, desert hikers often need to be amphibious. A great attraction of desert hiking is exploring canyons, where it's frequently necessary to wade or swim pools. The best footwear for canyoneering in warm weather are water shoes designed for river running. Sport sandals also work for some people, though they offer less protection from rocks and cactus spines than shoes.

Your feet will sweat in the desert, and heat and moisture buildup in your shoes or boots can cause blisters. The old hiker's trick of wearing two pairs of socks works well. The thick outer sock provides cushioning, and the thin liner sock clings to your skin and prevents the outer sock from rubbing and causing blisters. Wool or wool blends are hard to beat for the outer sock, because it retains its loft better than synthetics or cotton when damp with sweat. Synthetic liner socks do an excellent job of wicking sweat away from your skin. Other hikers prefer a single medium-weight wool blend or synthetic sock, especially in hot weather.

Sport sandals are excellent around camp.

If you're caught in cold, wet weather with non-waterproof boots, wear a pair of plastic bags over your outer socks as a vapor barrier. Gallon-size freezer bags with zipper closures work well, and also double as resealable trash bags. Although some moisture will build up from perspiration, your feet will be warmer than they would be if your socks were completely soaked.

WALKING STICKS AND TREKKING POLES

Trekking poles are very popular, and they do help maintain balance on rough trails and hiking cross-country. But I dislike having two sticks because it makes rock scrambling awkward. And I like having one hand free for photography. A single walking stick still turns you from an unstable biped into a stable tripod. The stick can also be used to push brush and low branches out of the way, to probe potential hiding areas during snake season, as a prop to turn a pack into a backrest, or to support a tarp for shelter from the weather.

Get rubber feet for your trekking poles or hiking stick. Rubber grips stony desert trails much better than steel or carbide, and it's also quiet. There's nothing quite as obnoxious as a large party of hikers with metal-tipped poles clickety-clacking up a trail like a giant metal centipede. And they'll never see any wildlife!

CLOTHING

Casual day hikers traveling in good weather can make do with nearly any durable clothing, but if you like to explore in changeable weather or stay out for several days on a backpacking trip, you'll find that technical outdoor clothing greatly increases your pleasure and safety. Technical clothing is made from synthetic fibers or a wool-synthetic blend. Both dry quickly,

Use the walking stick loop to hang the stick from
your wrist when you need both hands.

TIP

Attach a small loop of nylon cord to the top of your walking stick. The loop lets you hang the stick from your wrist when you need both hands for a moment. It also makes it easier to attach a tarp to create shelter from rain or sun.

---

wick moisture away from your skin, and are designed for use in layers.

Some desert hikers prefer to wear long-sleeved shirts and pants even in hot weather, for protection from the sun and thorny plants. Others, including the author, like to hike in short sleeves and shorts as much as possible. Zip-off hiking pants that convert to shorts are a great weight-saving compromise, and long-sleeved hiking shirts usually have sleeves that can be rolled up and secured.

The "four-layer" system is versatile enough to handle nearly any weather condition and also helps keep your load light. The first, inner layer consists of lightweight, synthetic, moisture-wicking long underwear. A pair of sturdy pants (with shorts as a warm-weather option) and a sturdy shirt that will hold up to brush and rocks forms the second layer. The third layer consists of an insulating jacket or parka. The

---

TIP

When wearing shorts, don't forget to use sunscreen on your arms and legs!

---

fourth layer consists of a good set of rain pants and jacket with hood. If this outer layer is constructed from a waterproof and breathable fabric, then it will do double duty as a wind shell.

Protect your head. In cold weather, up to half your body heat loss is through your head, because of all the blood vessels close to your skin. For the same reason, protect your head from summer sun with a good sun hat. Some hikers like floppy, broad-brimmed cotton hats; others like the "desert rat" style with a long flap in the back. Whatever the style, it should not only keep the sun out of your eyes but also shade your neck and ears. Baseball-style caps are only a little better than no hat at all.

Except in summer, don't forget a pair of fleece gloves. Desert mornings can be very cold, and packing up camp with numb fingers is unpleasant.

Down is the lightest and most durable insulation, and is very practical in the desert. Down used to lose its insulating value if it got really soaked, but modern down is treated to make it water repellent. Still, if you're going to be hiking in sustained very wet conditions (which can happen in the desert in the winter), carry a synthetic fleece jacket. Even when soaked, fleece can be wrung out and worn immediately.

Don't put up with being overheated or chilled. While hiking, stop to add or subtract layers as necessary to stay comfortable. As soon as you stop, add layers to keep warm in cool weather, or seek out shade in hot weather.

FOOD

You should bring some food on all but the shortest hikes. High-calorie food keeps your energy levels high. Sandwiches are always good on day hikes, or you can bring fruit, cheese, crackers, nuts, and drink mixes.

This is a good place to shoot down the myth that dehydrated food doesn't make sense for desert backpacking. Since you have to carry water anyway, why not save a step and carry fully hydrated food? But hydrated food means either fresh food, which doesn't keep, or canned food, which is heavy and leaves you carrying the empty cans for the entire trip. And many desert hikes have enough springs and other water sources so you don't have to carry a huge load of water all the time. Although a great deal of specialty dehydrated food is made for backpacking and lightweight camping, it is very expensive. Many items found in supermarkets make good backpacking food at lower cost. Using just supermarket food, I have been able to do many backpacking trips with no more than 1.5 pounds of food per person per day.

Of course, on a day hike you can carry sandwiches, fresh fruit and other fresh food. A juicy, sweet orange is a real delight on a hot summer hike!

For breakfast on backpacking trips: low-bulk cold cereals with powdered milk, hot cereals, dried fruit, breakfast bars, hot chocolate, tea, and coffee bags. For lunch: munchies such as nuts, cheese, crackers, dried fruit, candy bars, athletic energy bars, dried soup, hard candy, beef or turkey jerky, sardines, and fruit-flavored drink mixes. For dinner: dried noodle or rice-based dishes supplemented with margarine and possibly a small can of tuna, turkey, or chicken.

On some multiday trips, water has to be carried for dry camps. In this case, plan to use minimum-water foods. By that, I mean foods that need little or no excess water to prepare or clean up. Macaroni, for

---

TIP

I like to keep an athletic energy bar or two in my pack so I always have something to eat even if I don't take anything else.

TIP

On hot-weather trips, avoid chocolate and other foods that melt easily. Also avoid foods that spoil easily, like the softer varieties of cheese.

---

example, requires extra water for cooking. Avoid frying or other cooking that requires water for cleanup.

On warmer trips or when you'll have to carry a lot of water, consider leaving your stove behind and eating trail munchies and other food that doesn't require cooking.

Before leaving home, remove excess packaging such as cardboard boxes. Plastic bags with zipper closures make excellent food repackaging bags. Messy items should be double bagged. Pack margarine and peanut butter in reliable, wide-mouth plastic jars (available from outdoor suppliers). Unless you really trust the seal, put the container in a plastic bag also! Extra bags are useful during the trip for double bagging messy trash such as sardine cans. Zipper bags make good trash bags because the airtight seal minimizes food odors.

Dedicate one or more nylon stuff sacks to food storage; don't use them for anything else during the

---

TIP

Since water is usually the heaviest item in your pack, keep it close to your back for better balance. Don't put large amounts of water at the bottom or top of your pack.

---

trip. The idea is to confine food odors as much as possible to avoid attracting rodents and other animals. Although bears are not a problem in most desert areas, mice, squirrels, skunks, and ringtail cats can wreak havoc on your food supply.

On backpacking trips in reasonable weather (cool nights, warm days), use your pack and its contents as a sort of insulated cooler to keep food cool. When loading your pack in the morning, place food bags deep within your pack bag, and insulate them with a down or fleece jacket. Try to keep your pack in the shade during rest stops. The temperature in the shade is usually many degrees cooler than in the strong desert sun.

PACKS

Surprise! Ventilation is important when choosing a pack for desert use. Internal-frame packs dominate the market for good reason. Well-designed internal-frame packs ride closer to your body and have a lower center of gravity, which means the pack stays with your movements when you're negotiating rough terrain. For desert use, make sure your pack provides mesh panels against your back, or otherwise provides for air circulation.

Desert day hikers often prefer fanny packs because they keep your back cooler than a day pack. The major drawback is that sometimes you can't carry enough water in a fanny pack.

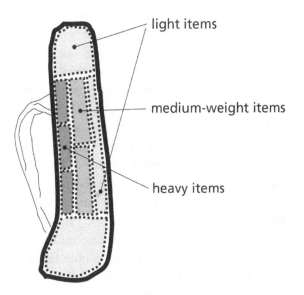

light items

medium-weight items

heavy items

Cross section of a properly loaded internal-frame pack

Avoid carrying water bottles outside your pack in hot weather, because the sun heats the water. Sunlight also rots plastic bottles and makes them brittle.

SHELTER

Many desert backpackers prefer to sleep under the stars when they can. In the dry, clear desert air, the horizon-to-horizon blaze of stars is an unforgettable sight. Still, deserts do have periods of rainy, snowy, or cold and windy weather when shelter is necessary. Also, sleeping on the ground is not advisable during the warmer months. In hot weather, most desert creatures, including snakes and insects, are nocturnal, and a floored and completely zippered net tent or three-season tent is comforting. As for use anywhere, sound construction and high quality is important. Don't get a winter mountaineering tent—they are designed to withstand heavy snow and high wind, and are too heavy and poorly ventilated for desert use. During cooler months when the nocturnal hunters are inactive, you may prefer to carry something lighter than a tent.

A net tent, in which all or part of the canopy is replaced by fine no-see-um netting, is often the ideal desert shelter. A conventional, waterproof fly covers the net canopy in the event of bad weather but can be left off (but not left behind!) during most desert nights.

Some experienced desert hikers avoid the weight and expense of a tent by carrying a nylon tarp with a separate groundsheet. A tarp provides good weather protection if set up properly and is versatile enough to use as a sunshade or windbreak during lunch stops. Remember that a tarp provides no protection from mosquitoes and other insects! Using a tarp effectively does take some practice. Consider that you may have no trees with which to pitch your tarp.

Another tent alternative, especially for solo hikers, is the bivouac sack. These are usually made of a single layer of waterproof and breathable fabric, such

A net tent without fly is often the ideal desert shelter.

as GORE-TEX. Designs range from simple sleeping bag covers with a bit of netting over the opening to one-man tents. Weights are similar to that of tarps. Bivi sacks are more secure in bad weather than tarps, but claustrophobic.

The midday desert sun is intense and quickly rots nylon tents and tarps. If you have to leave your

A tarp set up between a boulder and a walking stick is a good lightweight option but requires some practice.

TIP

A walking stick can do double duty as a tarp pole. Or, you may be able to use large boulders as supports.

shelter up all day, try to place it in the shade. Otherwise, take it down for the day and put it back up in the evening. The low-angle sun at morning and evening does little damage to nylon.

SLEEPING BAGS

A three-season bag is good for most desert hiking. In summer, you can use an even lighter bag.

If you sleep warm, you may wish to get a lighter bag, and if you sleep cold, you'll probably prefer a warmer bag.

Down is a very practical insulation for desert sleeping bags. High-quality down fill, though expensive, is still unsurpassed in insulating capability for its weight, and most down is now processed to make it water repellent. Since it is more durable, down is actually less expensive than synthetics over the lifetime of the bag.

Your choice of a sleeping bag presents an opportunity to save a lot of weight, often several pounds. My current bag is warm to about 10°F and weighs 1 pound 14 ounces.

Synthetic-fill sleeping bags are cheaper but much heavier and bulkier than down. They do have the advantage of being hypoallergenic.

SLEEPING PADS

Since lightweight sleeping bags don't provide much insulation or padding underneath, you'll need a sleeping pad. The best type currently available is the self-inflating foam-filled air mattress. These are less prone to punctures than a traditional air mattress, are much warmer, and at least as comfortable. Closed-cell foam pads are a cheaper alternative. They insulate very well and don't puncture, but they are not especially comfortable.

To check your self-inflating mattress before a trip, roll it up as tightly as you can, close the valve securely, then let it sit overnight. If it unrolls, it has pinhole leaks.

The hardest part of repairing tiny cactus spine punctures in a self-inflating mattress (the kind of holes that take half the night to let you down) is finding them. Blow up the pad as hard as you can by mouth, then sit on it in still water or in a bathtub.

TIP

Check very carefully for spines and thorns before laying out your mattress, and always use a groundsheet or a tent floor under it.

Look for tiny streams of bubbles and mark all the leaks with a pencil. Dry the pad, then repair the holes with the repair kit made by the manufacturer. I find that a good, flexible contact cement also works well. This tip is best used at home, but I have done it in the field!

2

Trip Planning

Always plan your trip itinerary carefully, especially for longer trips into remote areas. Leave a copy of your itinerary with a responsible person who will call the appropriate rescue authority if you are overdue by a specific amount of time. This is critical for solo trips, and important even when traveling with a group. Always notify your responsible person as soon as you return, to avoid a costly and unnecessary search attempt.

Increasingly, land-management agencies are no longer able to provide trip checkout services, even in national parks. Don't count on this service—use a reliable friend or family member.

The authority responsible for search and rescue in most western states is the local county sheriff, except in national parks, where the US National Park Service is the responsible agency. Agencies such as the US Forest Service and the Bureau of Land Management cooperate with search-and-rescue efforts on the lands they manage.

TIP

Don't hike solo in the desert, especially in remote areas or hot weather, unless you are experienced. Even then, plan and hike more cautiously than you would with a group.

Be sure everyone in the group knows the trip plan, including the approach route and meeting points if more than one vehicle will be used. If the group will separate on the hike, make sure each group has a map and a copy of the trip plan.

MAPS

Maps are essential for desert trip planning and for routefinding during the hike. Trails are rare in many desert hiking areas, and those that are shown on the maps may be little used, faint, and hard to find.

Atlases

Map atlases are available that cover an entire western state. These are helpful for getting an overview of an area and for finding the approach road. Some atlases are vague about backroads, and roads are built and abandoned frequently in some areas, so use caution.

National Forest/BLM Maps

The US Forest Service and the Bureau of Land Management publish maps of the areas they manage. Although these maps are usually planimetric and therefore don't show terrain features, they are excellent road maps. Backroads are shown as maintained, unmaintained (two-track), and four-wheel drive on most of these maps. Agency road numbers are also shown; national forest road junctions are generally signed with these numbers.

USGS Topographic Maps

The 7.5 minute series of topographic maps published by the US Geological Survey are the most detailed maps available. Each map covers an area of about 7 by 9 miles at a scale of 1:24,000, or 1 inch to 2,000 feet. Computerized methods are used to produce these extremely accurate maps from aerial photography. The sheer number of maps makes it difficult to revise them very often. Trails, roads, and other manmade features may be shown incorrectly. Also, don't rely on springs and permanent streams shown on USGS maps unless you can confirm their presence with a ranger, another experienced outdoor person, or a guidebook. These maps are available as paper copies from outdoor retailers and directly from USGS at ngmdb.usgs.gov/topoview/. Using the Topo Viewer, you can look at maps online, order paper copies, and download free digital copies.

Wilderness and Recreation Maps

Land-management agencies and private companies publish maps for certain popular desert wilderness and recreation areas. If available, these are often the best maps for the area, because they show an entire wilderness or park on one map, and are updated fairly frequently. Also, local backcountry regulations and guidelines are often shown. The most comprehensive series are the Trails Illustrated maps published by National Geographic.

Digital Maps

Recreation maps are available as web-based applications and smartphone apps. The best of these have many different map layers to choose from, including USGS topo maps, Trails Illustrated maps, US Forest Service and US National Park Service maps, satellite and aerial imagery, wildfire history, and much more. Trip planning tools let you map out trails, save waypoints for GPS use, and synchronize with your smartphone or upload to a dedicated GPS receiver. My current favorites are CalTopo.com and GaiaGPS.com.

GUIDEBOOKS

Hiking and backcountry guidebooks can be a valuable source of specific information. They are especially useful when you explore a new area for the first time. Check the revision date to make sure the book is reasonably up to date.

AGENCY INFORMATION

Before planning a desert hiking trip, check with the government agency having jurisdiction over the area. Rangers can often provide you with up-to-date road, trail, and water information, as well as maps.

OTHER INFORMATION SOURCES

Hiking clubs and individuals who are experienced in an area can often supply valuable tips.

Don't rely on information from a person that you don't know. Check his or her knowledge by asking a question to which you already know the answer. Such care is especially important when gathering information about water sources.

3

Approaches

DESERT BACKROAD ROUTEFINDING

Popular desert hiking areas have well-signed access roads and trailheads, but little-used areas may be more difficult to find. Review the approach at home ahead of time. Consider that road signs may be missing.

VEHICLE PREPARATION

A vehicle with reasonably high clearance and four-wheel or all-wheel drive is best for unmaintained desert backroads, though you can drive most maintained desert roads in almost any car, with care. If you're shopping for a new car, keep in mind that most sport utility and crossover vehicles are really designed for paved road use, despite their appearance. Look for a stiffer suspension, higher clearance, and all-weather tires for your desert ride. Also make sure the vehicle comes with a full-sized spare tire.

When exploring remote areas and especially in hot weather, consider using more than one vehicle in case one breaks down.

Keep your vehicle reliable by practicing preventive maintenance. Fifty miles from the nearest garage is no place to have an old fan belt break. Before leaving home, check coolant and oil levels and tire pressure and condition. Don't forget to check your spare tire. Some desert drivers carry a can or two of tire repair/inflator. It can save the day if you pick up a nail.

Carry a tow chain or rope. Sometimes another car comes by but neither of you has a tow chain.

Carry extra water and food in your car in case you get stuck or stranded. Think in terms of being able to survive for several days, until searchers find you.

When leaving the last outpost of civilization for desert back roads, top off your fuel tank. Driving on sandy or rocky roads, and using four-wheel drive, uses more fuel than highway or city driving.

TIP

Keep a set of basic tools, including a sturdy shovel, in your car, and learn how to use them. In sandy areas, consider carrying sand mats, made from old pieces of carpet.

DRIVING DESERT ROADS

Road maintenance is often infrequent on desert dirt roads. Washouts, potholes, deep sand, ruts, and other obstacles can appear suddenly, so watch your speed. Deep sand is a hazard on some approach roads; a four-wheel-drive vehicle may be necessary.

Desert land is easily scarred by vehicle tracks; the evidence from irresponsible off-highway vehicle use, four-wheeling, and desert vehicle racing will be visible for many years. Stay on the established roadway, whether it's a maintained road or a two-track. And needless to say, those of us who enjoy exploring wild, roadless areas will respect all road closures and signs.

If you have to turn around on a desert road, remember that the shoulders may be very soft. Turn around by making several short turns and remaining on the traveled or maintained surface.

Drive slowly on rough roads. If in doubt about an especially bad section, or a drop-off that you can't see, check it out on foot. Don't hesitate to do a little rock moving and roadwork if needed. Also, low speed lets you stop if you start to lose traction. Most times, you'll be able to back out if you do it carefully. Getting stuck is an inevitable part of desert driving, but if you're prepared, being stuck doesn't have to be a major problem.

If you can't move with gentle application of power, stop. Don't try to power out—you'll just dig yourself into a hole. If you have four-wheel drive and got stuck while you are in two-wheel drive, shift into four-wheel drive and gently try to move out. If that fails, get out and analyze the situation. If you're traveling with another vehicle, the quickest solution is usually to have the other machine tow you out. If that's not practical, or yours is the only vehicle, then you'll have a bit more work to do. If the wheels have sunk into soft sand but the vehicle is not high centered, you may be able to get out by digging the sand away from the tires so you can move with minimum power. Sand mats will help maintain traction—rubber floor mats can also be used for this purpose. If you're high centered, then jack up the wheels one at a time, fill in the hole, and lay down your sand mats or other firm material (brush can work well) under the tire and back in the direction you need to go. Once all is ready, carefully ease back onto firm ground.

Using sand mats to get a vehicle unstuck

Flooded roads can have hidden washouts that
might wash away a vehicle.

Don't cross flooded washes. The roadbed may be
eroded away, and the water is probably much deeper
and swifter than it appears. One foot of swift-moving
water can wash away even a high-clearance vehicle.
Don't park your vehicle in a dry wash or streambed,
especially during the late-summer thunderstorm season. A distant storm that you're completely unaware
of may cause the wash to flash flood without warning.

Flooding from summer thunderstorms usually
subsides in a few hours. On the other hand, flooding
can be prolonged for days if caused by heavy winter
or spring rain, especially if melting snow in the high
country adds to the runoff.

TIP

*Consider that washes you crossed on
the way to the trailhead might
be flooding and be impossible to
cross on the way out.*

In some desert areas, severe dust storms can occur that may suddenly reduce visibility to zero. These are more of a hazard at high speed on freeways and highways than on backroads. If you encounter suddenly reduced visibility, drive completely clear of the roadway and turn off all lights. Many accidents occur when panicked drivers stop suddenly in the traffic lane. If you leave your lights on, even if you're clear of the road, other drivers may see your lights and steer toward them, thinking you're on the road. In addition, wind-driven sand can seriously damage windshield glass and body paint. You can minimize this damage by stopping until the wind abates.

4

On the Trail

USING MAP AND COMPASS

Desert hiking, which sometimes involves faint trails and cross-country hiking, demands a lot of your map-reading skills. With practice and experience, you should be able to visualize the terrain in three dimensions by looking at a topographic map.

The best way to learn to read a topographic map is to use one for an area you already know. By comparing the features of the terrain with its depiction on the map, you'll quickly master the art of map reading.

Contour lines are the key feature of topographic maps. Each line represents a constant elevation above sea level. Where the terrain is gentle, the lines are spread apart. Closely spaced contour lines mean that the terrain is steep. Ridges and drainages are shown by U- or V-shaped lines. Drainages are usually distinguished by thin blue dashed or solid lines representing an intermittent or permanent stream.

Contour lines that are missing mean there is a vertical or overhanging cliff. It's especially important to

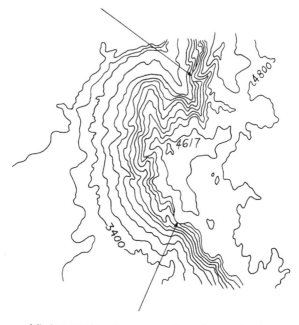

Missing contour lines mean there's a vertical or
overhanging cliff.

note missing contours along narrow canyon bottoms,
which usually means there's one or more pour-offs or
dry waterfalls. You may or may not be able to find a
route around these obstacles.

Learn the symbols used on your topographic map.
Wilderness and recreation area maps usually have
a legend or symbol guide printed on the map. The
US Geological Survey provides map user guides at
ngmdb.usgs.gov/topoview/.

Don't rely on permanent streams that are shown on maps of desert country. They may not be reliable sources of water. Often maps show seasonal water that just happened to be present when the map was made. The same is true of springs.

Learn the difference between **true north**, as used on maps, and **magnetic north**, the direction your compass needle points. True north is the direction to the earth's geographic North Pole. Compass needles align themselves with the earth's magnetic field, and generally point toward a spot in northeastern Canada about a thousand miles from the geographic pole. **Declination** (also called variation) is the difference between true and magnetic north. Because the magnetic field changes slowly, declination changes with time. Good maps show the declination as of publication date as well as the rate of change. Declination can be as much as 16 or 17 degrees in the western United States, which will cause large errors if you don't correct for it. (There's yet a third north, grid north, which is the difference between the grid lines on the map and true north. For fieldwork, you can ignore it. In most cases, it's only a fraction of a degree.)

To help you relate the map to the landscape around you, orient the map and yourself toward true north. All good maps are printed with north toward the top of the sheet as a standard. Use your compass to determine north. Locate visible terrain features on the map, keeping in mind that desert objects are often much farther away than they appear. After you become familiar with the country, you'll be able to relate the map to terrain features without orienting it.

Triangulation can be used to identify unknown landmarks, such as mountain peaks. Take a compass bearing on the landmark, and then plot the bearing on your map, starting from your position. Use a protractor or the baseplate of your compass. Remember that you're working with magnetic bearings **to** the landmarks. The line will run through the unknown landmark. If the bearing line crosses several possible landmarks, hike a bit farther and take another bearing. The two lines will intersect at the landmark.

Resection (often incorrectly called triangulation) can be used if you are unsure of your position but have one or more known landmarks in sight. Take a bearing on each of the landmarks. If you have a single landmark to work with, you'll at least know that your position is along the bearing line. If you also know that you're on a linear feature, such as a trail, road, ridge, or drainage, then the point where the bearing line crosses that feature on your map is your position. If you're not along a defined linear feature, then take at least three bearings. They will cross and form a small triangle on your map—you are located within this "error triangle."

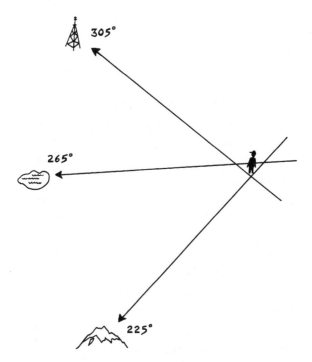

305°

265°

225°

Resection with map and compass can be
used if you are unsure of your position but
have at least two, and preferably three,
known landmarks in sight.

A compass with a sighting mirror makes triangulation bearings more accurate, and an adjustable
declination setting lets you work with true bearings
without having to correct for magnetic variation. The
type of compass with a clear plastic baseplate and a
rotating bearing ring works well for plotting bearing

lines on a map. Use the straight edge of another map to extend the compass straight edge if necessary.

USING SATELLITE NAVIGATION

A Global Positioning Receiver (GPS) can make desert routefinding easier, especially on unmarked roads that cross open desert valleys or plateaus with few landmarks. Because it uses satellites to determine your location and is unaffected by weather or darkness, GPS can help navigate when landmarks are poor or not visible.

When planning a hike where you know finding the trailhead or departure point will be difficult, use the map to determine the coordinates of the trailhead. Enter these coordinates in your GPS unit ahead of time. Then, as you drive the backroads, the GPS receiver will tell you which way to turn to keep heading toward the trailhead.

TIP

It may also be useful to enter the coordinates of your turnoff from the highway or major road if you suspect that it's unmarked. That can save a lot of time hunting up and down the highway for an obscure turnoff.

If your vehicle is not at an actual trailhead or other well-defined point, it might be hard to find on your return. Use the GPS to record the position before leaving for your hike. This technique is especially time saving when you have to park several miles out in a desert valley and hike to the foot of the mountains. The lower slopes (known as a "bajada") are often laced with numerous parallel washes and low ridges that all look the same. It also helps to park on a ridge rather than in a low spot, so you can spot your vehicle from a distance.

TRAIL WALKING

In hot weather, consider adopting the siesta system: Start hiking at first light; stop for a long break at around 10 a.m., or whenever the heat becomes too much. Rest in the shade, have a leisurely lunch, then start hiking again when the blast furnace abates. This can be as late as 5 p.m. in very hot weather. You can get in 7 or 8 hours of hiking during long summer days while avoiding the worst of the heat.

Before leaving your vehicle, whether you'll be hiking on trail or cross-country, look at your map and pick a baseline. This can be a road that borders one side of the area, a canyon rim, or any other feature that would be impossible to miss. Then, if you become completely disoriented, you can hike in the general direction of your baseline with the assurance

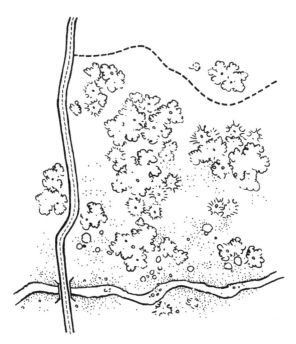

Picking baselines will make you more confident
in your explorations.

that you will eventually reach it. Of course, hiking to your baseline is a last resort because it may take you many miles out of your way. But having a known baseline will make you more confident in your explorations.

As you hike, stay oriented by paying attention to your direction of travel in relation to the position of the sun, wind direction, and slope of the ground and other terrain features.

If the group plans to split up, there should be an experienced desert hiker in each group. Agree on a meeting place and time, allowing extra time for delays, and make every effort to be there on time.

Well-traveled trails are easy to follow, and usually have good signs at the junctions. Most popular desert hiking areas have several good trails, and a larger network of little-used trails. It takes some skill to follow faint trails that may be confused by animal trails or disappear at drainage or side canyon crossings.

When trying to stay on a faint trail, note how the trail deals with streambed crossings and side canyons. Once you begin to see the pattern, you'll be able to pick out the trail on the far side before crossing.

Trail signs are often missing in remote desert areas where there is little money for trail maintenance. Refer to your map often and remain aware of your position and direction of travel.

Rock cairns are commonly used to mark trails and routes in areas without trees. Trail crews usually build large, solid cairns. Treat smaller cairns with a healthy dose of skepticism—the person who built the cairn may have been off route themselves.

When following a cairned trail or route, always spot the next cairn before leaving sight of the last.

TIP
At dusk, keep an eye out for rattlesnakes, because they are active in the evening during hot weather.

If necessary, walk expanding circles around the last cairn to find the next.

CROSS-COUNTRY HIKING
Although many hikers are reluctant to leave well-traveled trails, open desert country invites off-trail exploration and it can be very rewarding. However, cross-country hiking takes responsibility for your route from the trail builders and puts it squarely on your shoulders. For example, are ridges the best route of travel because drainages tend to be choked with brush? Or are the ridges interrupted by frequent rock outcrops that must be circumvented? The best way to gain this type of knowledge is through experience on trails in the area.

Many desert wildernesses have no trails at all. In this case, hike some of the trails in a similar area before graduating to completely trackless areas.

Note how the trail builder routed the trail as you learn the general character of the region.

Use your map to pick the best route through the terrain, considering obstacles.

Game trails made by deer, wild burros, and wild horses can make travel a lot easier if the trail goes in the direction you want to travel.

In desert canyon or mountain country, the classic orienteering technique of following a compass bearing (or a GPS course) directly to your destination rarely works. Obstacles such as steep rocky slopes or cliffs, areas of heavy brush, and deep canyons usually make it impossible to follow a straight line.

Pick a distant, unmistakable landmark near your destination or in the direction you want to go. Then, as you deviate around obstacles, use the landmark to maintain your general direction of travel. A GPS receiver can be used the same way, by setting a waypoint at your destination.

Don't try to use a GPS receiver while on the move—you should be watching for rattlesnakes, cactus, and other hazards as you move. Instead, turn it on at rest stops to get an update on your progress and the direction to your goal.

TIP

When hiking without a map, make sure you know the location of your vehicle. Park near a prominent landmark or along a well-traveled road.

Though it's always safer to have a good map of the area, it's sometimes very rewarding to explore an area without one.

Never enter an area without a map unless you've selected a good baseline to walk to if all else fails.

As you hike, look back often to keep track of your return route. Landmarks change shape and appearance as you move, and as the lighting changes during the day.

A small pair of binoculars can be very useful for routefinding, because they allow you to check out terrain from a distance before you're committed to a route.

CANYON HIKING

Some deserts such as those in the plateau country of southern Utah and northern Arizona feature deep, narrow canyons. These have their own special challenges. At least staying on the route is simple, especially if you're hiking downstream. But it can be very difficult to determine how far you've progressed. One way to do this is to keep your map available so you can get it without taking off your pack and use it to keep track of each twist and turn as you hike.

Narrow canyons can flash flood without warning. Numerous hikers have lost their lives in flooded canyons; always check the weather forecast carefully before entering a narrow canyon. See page 49 for more information.

When you're planning a canyon hike, note distinct landmarks, such as side canyons, on the map. On the hike, watch for your predetermined landmarks and note the time on the map as you reach each one. Soon you'll have a good idea of your rate of travel.

An accurate altimeter can be used with a detailed topographic map to track your progress in very narrow canyons. The altimeter should be temperature-compensated and read in 20-foot increments to match the accuracy of the map. Cheap altimeters that read in 100-foot increments or larger are useless for this purpose.

Don't count on a GPS receiver for canyon bottom navigation, because often there aren't enough satellites in view for the unit to get a fix.

Smaller canyons and side canyons are often choked with obstacles. These include pools of standing water

---

TIP

A lightweight air mattress is a good way to float your pack across pools. If the water is too cold to wade or swim, you can use a small pack raft.

---

that may be too deep or cold to wade. Chockstones often partially block narrow canyons, forming pour-offs—dry waterfalls that may be impossible to bypass without technical climbing gear. Other canyons may have permanent streams that must be constantly waded.

GETTING LOST AND FOUND

It's rare to become totally lost if you make an effort to be aware of your surroundings. More commonly, hikers become apprehensive when an expected land-mark, trail junction, or their vehicle doesn't appear when expected.

Don't hesitate to ask another hiker for directions, even in heavily used areas. The moment you become unsure of your position, stop. Take a rest break, have some water and food, and make a conscious effort to relax. Panic is the usual cause of people becoming seriously lost. Continuing blindly onward is a guar-anteed way to make the situation worse.

Take stock of your overall situation. If on a day hike, are you about to be caught by darkness? If so, do you have extra clothing, food, and water? If on a backpacking trip, can you camp where you are? Does bad weather threaten? Is there a group member who's exhausted or has an injury or a medical problem? Take care of the most important things one at a time.

TIP

*Climb to a nearby hill or ridge and
look for familiar landmarks.*

If you're following a faint trail or cairned route,
look around for signs of the trail or the next cairn.
The trail may have taken an unexpected sharp turn.
Use your stopping point as a base for the search.

Look for unique landmarks and use those to locate
yourself on your map.

If you can't locate the trail, then if possible backtrack to your last known point—a cairn, section of
trail that's distinct, or a tree blaze.

As a last resort, walk to your predetermined baseline. If you choose a good baseline, you'll eventually
arrive at it, though at the cost of being hours or days
late. Carefully consider the terrain you'll have to traverse to reach your baseline.

The classic advice to follow a drainage or a river
downstream to civilization may not always work
in desert wilderness. For example, the canyonlands
country of southern Utah is broken by narrow canyons that are often extremely deep and impossible
to enter without technical climbing gear. In the cen-
tral mountains of Arizona, canyon bottoms often
are blocked by dry waterfalls and deep pools. These

obstacles make travel rough and slow, or even impossible without special equipment. In such areas, ridges usually offer the easiest traveling. In the desert ranges of Nevada, southeastern California, and western Arizona, traveling downhill will take you to a highway or well-traveled dirt road, but you will be descending into hotter, drier country. Be sure you have enough water and endurance before attempting such a walk. In certain places, roads are built along ridgelines above canyon wilderness areas, and the best tactic is to follow ridges uphill.

Emergency Signals

If you're completely disoriented, or an injury prevents you from traveling, then stay put and signal. Assuming that you let someone responsible know your plans before the trip, then searchers will eventually find you. You can help them find you more quickly by signaling. In North America, three of anything is the universal distress signal. You can use three fires, smoke columns, light flashes, or blasts on a whistle.

If you have a signal mirror, use it even if you haven't spotted a search vehicle or aircraft. In the desert, a mirror flash can be seen for at least 50 miles on a sunny day. Flash at any aircraft you spot, and regularly sweep the horizon with the mirror. Even if no one is searching for you, you'll eventually attract attention.

Consider carrying a personal locator beacon (PLB) if you hike alone or in remote areas. PLBs are similar to the emergency locator beacons carried on boats and aircraft, except much smaller and lighter. When activated, a PLB determines your precise location via its built-in GPS receiver, then transmits this data to the search-and-rescue satellites (SARSAT) orbiting overhead, which then relay the data to a rescue coordination center. Because you must register your PLB, with minutes of activation the rescue center not only knows your location, but your name and contact information. If the center can't contact you, rescue is automatically initiated.

Cellular phones are worth carrying for emergency purposes, but their battery life is short and you may not be able to get a signal in remote areas. The cell system is designed to cover highways and urban areas, but not wilderness where there is no permanent human presence. Leave your phone off in the backcountry, both to save the battery for an emergency, and also to avoid annoying fellow hikers who are in the wilderness to escape from human noise and complications.

RESPONSIBLE HIKING

The desert, though it gives an initial impression of being a tough landscape, is actually fragile. Widely spaced plants and elusive wildlife are adapted to unforgiving climate conditions and often have a tenuous hold on life. When the desert is scarred, it takes a long time to recover. With a little care and common sense, we desert hikers can minimize the damage we do.

Don't feed or molest animals or damage plants. You'll often come across prehistoric and historic ruins, rock drawings, and artifacts. Never disturb them, whether made by Native Americans or immigrant prospectors. As part of our shared culture, such sites are protected by state and federal law.

If you're following a trail, stay on it. Don't cut switchbacks or take other shortcuts. Desert trails don't receive much maintenance, so shortcuts tend to become established. Such false trails can mislead other hikers and increase erosion of fragile desert soil. And, as experienced hikers know, shortcutting uses more energy than staying on the trail.

When hiking cross-country, keep on less fragile areas as much as practical. Gravel wash bottoms often form good routes through desert mountain ranges, for example. In canyon country, rock outcrops often form terraces that can be followed.

Many hikers own dogs and like to take them hiking. Be considerate of wildlife and other hikers by following the rules. National forests and state parks generally require that dogs be kept on leashes.

National parks almost always prohibit dogs on trails and in the backcountry.

In camp, keep your dog under control and don't allow it to bark. Barking disturbs other campers as well as wildlife.

Avoid taking your dog into areas with cholla cactus, unless you know that it's smart enough to avoid cactus. One experience with removing the barbed spines from the paws and mouth of a very unhappy pet is usually enough to convince people to leave the dog at home.

Cryptobiotic Soil

Cryptobiotic soil is the black, crusty layer that often forms on the surface in sandy areas. It's a combination of mosses, lichens, and bacteria in a dependent relationship that acts to bind the sandy soil together and slow down erosion. The crust takes many years to reform once disturbed. Avoid cryptobiotic soil wherever possible—stay on the sandy areas between, or on bedrock.

Some land managers recommend that groups spread out when hiking cross-country instead of walking single file, to avoid creating trails.

Meeting Other Hikers

Sound carries a long way in the open desert. Respect other hikers' desire for solitude by avoiding loud conversations and noise. Choose pack and clothing colors that blend in to the desert's muted colors. As mentioned earlier, use rubber-tipped hiking sticks to avoid the obnoxious clatter of metal-tipped poles.

Meeting Horses and Pack Animals

Some desert trails traverse very steep terrain with drop-offs, such as those in the Grand Canyon. Spooked animals can endanger themselves and their riders.

When meeting horses and pack animals on steep terrain, move downhill off the trail, or to the outside of bends or switchbacks, and stand quietly. Always follow instructions given by the packer.

Meeting Cyclists

Since cyclists are less maneuverable than you are, move off the trail for them. This avoids causing the cyclist to ride off trail, which creates tire ruts in fragile desert soil.

Human Waste

Desert country poses some special challenges for those who want to be considerate wilderness users. There's less open water to potentially contaminate, but human waste decomposes very slowly in dry, sandy soil. First of all, if bathroom facilities are

---

TIP

Carry used toilet paper and other hygiene items in doubled zipper bags, with a small amount of baking soda to absorb odor.

---

available (at trailheads and campgrounds, for example), use them! Otherwise, select a site at least 100 yards from streams, lakes, springs, and dry washes. If possible, avoid barren, sandy soil. Dig a small "cathole" about 6 inches down into the organic layer of the soil. When finished, refill the hole, making the site as natural as possible. Land managers now recommend that all toilet paper be carried out, and in some heavily used areas, all human waste as well.

A small plastic trowel makes it easier to dig holes and minimize damage to ground cover.

5

Desert Camping

PICKING YOUR CAMPSITE

There are many factors that help create a memorable campsite. Scenery is always near the top of the list. Most of us go into the backcountry looking for a degree of solitude and a feeling that we are in someplace truly wild. It goes without saying that desert hikers must practice "Leave No Trace" camping techniques in order to preserve the wilderness for future hikers. If you carried it in, you can carry it out.

To help preserve your own sense of wildness and that of others, choose a campsite that is screened from other campers and hikers. If you've been following a trail, move a couple of hundred yards away from it, and camp behind a low ridge, a rock outcrop, or a patch of brush.

Avoid campsites near rock piles, old buildings, pack rat nests, or other piles of debris. These are favorite sites for rodents who may decide your presence and your food supply signals a free dinner, and rodents attract rattlesnakes. Insects are also more common in such areas.

Don't camp near desert water sources unless you can't avoid it (in a narrow canyon, for example). Animals usually move to water at night, and your presence may prevent them from getting a much-needed drink. Also, the area around springs and natural water tanks tends to be heavily used. In Arizona, there's actually a state law that prohibits camping near a spring. Consider too that mice and other camp robbers are more numerous near water.

As an alternative, learn to dry camp. The technique will open up many superb campsites, such as rimrock areas, ridges, and even mountain peaks. To avoid having to carry a heavy load of water all day, plan to pass a reliable water source in late afternoon. Pick up enough water to camp and to reach the next reliable water source the next day. Start looking for a campsite whenever you feel like it, and camp wherever you like.

Camp on ground that resists damage. Sand, gravel, and rock ledges are excellent choices. As tempting as it might be, don't camp in desert flower fields or meadows during the wet season. Also avoid cryptobiotic soil. You'll want a reasonably level tent or bedsite, but don't excavate one, except in easily restored ground such as bare sand or gravel.

TIP

In a pinch, you may be able to find small level sites on the uphill sides of trees or boulders.

If rain or stormy weather threatens, pick a well-drained campsite. A gently sloping or slightly dome-shaped area keeps water from pooling under your tent. Look for absorbent ground, such as pine needles (there are trees in many desert mountain ranges!), sand, or gravel. Never dig drainage ditches around your campsite—this outdated practice causes too much damage to soil and slow-growing vegetation.

Never camp in dry washes or drainages below the flood level, even in apparently stable weather. Heavy rain falling miles away can turn your camp into a deadly torrent with very little warning. At best, you'll lose all your gear, and at worst, you may lose your life.

In warm weather, you may wish to site your camp so it is in the shade as long as possible in the morning. In cold weather, you'll probably want the sun to hit your frosty tent or sleeping bag as early as possible. You can simplify this process by using your compass (or a smartphone app such as the Photographer's Ephemeris) to measure the bearing on which the sun rises on the first day of the trip, making allowances if the horizon isn't flat. Then, when selecting your campsite during the evening, sight along the same bearing to predict where the sun will rise. Remember to allow for differences in the horizon.

Before leaving, restore your campsite to as natural a condition as you can. Carefully look for bits of litter and gear you may have dropped or forgotten. Level any tent or bed sites you may have dug out of sand or gravel, and use a dead piece of brush to whisk over your tracks.

CAMPFIRES

Campfires are part of the wilderness experience for many hikers, but the desert is not the place for campfires—there simply isn't enough wood in most areas. Some areas are closed to campfires by the land managers, and in others, a responsible hiker will see the scarcity of wood and choose not to build a fire. In lusher, higher desert country and desert mountain ranges, wood may be plentiful enough to justify an occasional fire.

During periods of high fire danger, campfires may not be allowed. Before your trip, check with the agency that manages your hiking area to see if any fire restrictions are in effect.

Keep your fire small and use as little wood as you can. Experienced hikers know that small fires are easier to cook on and easier to snuggle up to for warmth.

Collect only dead, downed wood. Never break wood from trees or brush. Desert trees grow very slowly—if there isn't enough wood on the ground, then the area is too heavily used to justify a campfire. Likewise, if you think you need a saw or ax to get wood, then don't build a fire.

If there's no firepit at your campsite, strongly consider doing without a fire. If you must have one, build a no-trace fire. Choose a sandy or nearly barren patch of soil in an area sheltered from wind. Sandy or gravelly wash bottoms are ideal because the next flood will wash the charcoal downstream and grind it up. But don't sleep there—put your camp up on the banks above the highest flood marks. Dig a pit about 2 feet in diameter and about a foot deep, using the soil from the pit to form a berm around it. Keep your fire small and confined within the pit. When you're breaking camp, mix sand or dirt with the ashes and stir until the coals are cool to the touch. When you're sure the fire is completely out, bury it using the dirt

---

TIP

Wherever possible, use existing firepits rather than building new ones. Fireplaces make scars that last for dozens of years in the dry climate.

TIP

Never use rocks to build a fireplace. This outdated practice results in campsites that are littered with ugly blackened stones, and stones can explode from the heat of the fire.

---

you excavated. Done properly, this technique hides all traces of the fire. After a bit of wind or rain, your former campsite will look pristine once again.

STOVES

A lightweight stove is a necessity on most desert backpacking trips. There are many good models from which to choose, and both gasoline and butane/propane stoves work well in desert climates. Avoid stoves fueled by pure butane—they don't work well on cold mornings.

If you use a butane/propane stove, don't count on buying more fuel canisters on a trip to a remote desert region. Take all you'll need from home.

It's common for stoves to become clogged with sand and dust on desert trips. Make sure you have a stove repair kit that includes a jet cleaner. Some stoves have built in jet cleaning mechanisms—these can save a lot of time and frustration.

In the desert, strong winds often blow for hours at a time, especially in the spring. Even a slight breeze greatly reduces the efficiency of an unprotected stove—which means you'll use a lot more fuel, and cooking takes longer. The effectiveness of the windscreen varies greatly from stove to stove.

Component stoves, in which the fuel tank is separated from the burner assembly, often have windscreens that completely enclose the burner. This design works very well and protects the flame even in strong winds. It also increases the efficiency of the stove, even in calm air.

Conventional stoves, designed with the burner and fuel tank as a single unit, are generally more convenient because they do not have to be assembled before use. The windscreen never encloses the burner completely, because doing so would allow too much heat to reach the fuel tank. To protect the stove from wind, you'll have to build a windbreak from your pack or other gear, or stones.

Never use any type of windscreen to completely enclose both the burner and fuel tank on any stove. The fuel tank can easily overheat and explode. During use, periodically check the temperature of the fuel tank. If the tank gets more than warm to the touch, turn the stove off.

RINGTAIL CATS AND OTHER
NIGHT VISITORS

Though few desert areas have bear problems, there are plenty of small- to medium-size critters, including mice, chipmunks, squirrels, and ringtail cats, that will doggedly chew through the toughest pack to get to the tempting aromas within. And although skunks don't generally attack your food, their leisurely explorations of your camp can keep you up all night. A few precautions will minimize the chance of gear damage or lost food.

By the way, ringtail cats are not cats at all, but a member of the raccoon family that is common in the American Southwest and much of Mexico. A bit smaller than a house cat, it has a fox-like face, with large eyes and ears. It has a tail about the same length as its body, with about 14 black and white rings. Ringtail cats are nocturnal and shy of humans, so they tend to investigate your camp after you're asleep, when they can be very adept at getting into your food.

Prepack your food in resealable zipper-type plastic bags so it can be closed up after use on the trail. Pack all food in large plastic or nylon bags, organized by meal or day, or whatever system you prefer. The large bags make it easier to remove all the food from your pack at night.

Avoid heavily used campsites when possible. At these sites, camp robber animals are used to humans and their food. Your arrival is the ringing of the dinner bell. At one popular desert campsite, my friend and I were greeted by a large, fearless striped skunk within minutes of our arrival at dusk. He walked right up to us as we were laying out our groundsheets, and it seemed to us that he had "Feed me!" written all over his face. We picked up our packs and hiked for another hour by headlamp rather than spend a sleepless night fending him off.

Never, never feed wild animals no matter how cute—you are not helping them, **you're killing them**. Either they get dependent on human food and then starve during the off-season, or they are killed by people who are angry at having their gear destroyed.

If you have trees in your campsite, hang your food sacks from a 10- or 15-foot-high tree limb, if possible. The most foolproof technique is to divide your food into two equal sacks. Use a stone to toss the end of a piece of nylon cord over the limb well out from the trunk, then tie half your food to the end. Pull the food up to the limb, then tie your remaining food sack onto the cord as high as you can reach. Stuff the excess cord into the food sack, then use a stick

---

TIP

If there aren't any trees, look for a couple of boulders you can use to support a length of nylon cord horizontally.

---

to push the second sack several feet higher than your head. The first sack will act as a counterweight and descend a few feet, but it should remain at least as high as the second sack. In the morning, use a stick to pull down one of the sacks. This method is proof against most animals, even bears, if the sacks are at least 10 feet above the ground. But any height you can achieve is better than leaving your food on the ground.

The top of a single boulder can be used to support a horizontal hiking stick or branch, extended into the air to one side. Weight the end of the stick with stones or jam it into a crack, then hang your food bags from the projecting end.

A party of three or more hikers (or two hikers with a pair of trekking poles each) can use walking sticks to make a tripod by lashing the tops together with cord. Since mice and other rodents can easily climb the sticks, hang your food bags low enough to be well away from the legs, but high enough so animals can't jump onto the sacks.

Hang your food bags to keep mice and
other night visitors out.

If there's nothing at all to hang your food from,
then you may have no choice but to leave it in your
pack. Close all the plastic food bags to minimize odor
but leave the food stuffsack open. Leave all the zip-
pers and closures open on your pack, so mice won't

chew a hole trying to get in. With luck, you'll only lose one or two of the more enticing items in your pack. Actually, if you camp in areas with little use, chances are you won't be bothered at all. Truly wild animals are very shy about approaching a human camp, so you generally won't have problems with camp robbers at little-used sites unless you camp in the same site for several days.

Another desert trick is to put your food bag right behind your head, or even use it as a pillow, on the theory that your close proximity will scare off the night marauders. It's probably even more effective if you snore! If nothing else, you have a better chance of hearing the little munchers and being able to run them off. Of course, you can lose a lot of sleep. This trick can backfire badly if a skunk invades your camp, and is extremely dangerous in bear country.

BREAKING CAMP

Everything you carry into wild areas **must be carried out.**

Never bury food scraps, packaging, or any sort of trash. Animals will dig up anything with a food odor, and in the dry climate, trash lasts just about forever.

Never burn trash in a campfire. Many packaging materials contain thin layers of aluminum, which does not burn in even the hottest campfire. Like

---

TIP

Repackage your food at home into resealable, zippered bags to minimize the amount of trash created on the trip.

---

plastic, it fuses into small blobs. Popular camping areas are scarred with numerous old firepits that glitter with bits of aluminum and plastic. Also, some plastics give off highly toxic fumes when burned.

Carry out some trash left by careless or thoughtless people. This is especially practical toward the end of your trip when your pack is light. Then you can bask in the glow of self-righteous pleasure!

6

Safety in the Desert

MINE SHAFTS

Desert areas have always been attractive to miners and prospectors because of the expanses of bare, often mineralized rock. As a result, abandoned mine shafts and prospect holes are common in some areas. While land managers and mining authorities are making an attempt to secure dangerous sites, the sheer vastness of the problem leaves a lot of hazards in the desert backcountry. **Never enter any mine shaft.** Besides the obvious hazards of falling and collapse, old mines often contain poisonous or radioactive gases, as well as unstable explosives and dangerous equipment. Report any explosives or other unusual hazards to the land-management agency after your trip.

When hiking through heavy brush, or at night, be especially alert for old mine shafts. In areas that have attracted a lot of prospecting, miners often dig numerous small pits. Even though these pits are usually only a few feet deep, coming upon one unaware can result in ankle or leg injuries or worse.

TIP

The presence of an old road, even if closed and now part of designated wilderness, may be a sign that there are old mines in the area.

In mined areas, stay away from the edges of vertical shafts, even if covered. The edges of shafts often continue to crumble for years after abandonment. Also avoid depressions in the ground—these may mark shafts or pits that have been covered with wood or metal that is rotting or rusting away.

WILDLIFE

Remember that you're a visitor when in wild desert country. Although humans have the responsibility to be careful stewards of the remaining wild lands and their animal and plant inhabitants, we are guests and should behave appropriately and respectfully. Most hazardous encounters with wild animals are a direct result of the human acting irresponsibly.

Never approach or attempt to handle any wild animal. All animals will defend themselves if they feel threatened or cornered. Even rabbits will bite to protect their young. By approaching or harassing wildlife, you are placing great stress on the animal and endangering yourself.

Mountain Lions

Cougars, as they are also known, are rare and elusive creatures in the remote country where they still survive. You'll be lucky to see tracks, let alone the animal. The only cases of attack have been when the human aroused the lion's predatory instincts by appearing to be prey. Running and mountain biking in lion country seems to have a slight chance of evoking the same response that a running deer causes.

If you do encounter a mountain lion, avoid prey-like reactions. Make yourself appear as big and threatening as possible, and make unnatural sounds, by rattling metal pots or the like. Don't turn your back on the animal, and don't run. Mountain lion encounters usually result in just a fleeting glimpse of this magnificent animal.

Wolves and Coyotes

Wolves have recently been reintroduced in some desert regions. They are not a hazard to humans. Neither are coyotes. The thrilling nocturnal howl of coyotes is as much a part of the desert as the clear, starry nights. We can only hope that the wolves are successful in their former ranges and that we will be lucky enough to hear their song as well.

Domestic Cattle

Much desert country is also used for grazing, so you're likely to encounter cattle. Generally, cattle are used to humans, and either avoid you or move away. It's possible that a bull could be dangerous, so it's a good idea to give cattle a reasonable margin as you pass them.

If you find the presence of cattle offensive in the backcountry, check with the land-management agency before your trip. Cattle are rotated to different grazing allotments at various times, and the rangers can tell you which areas to avoid. Also, you can avoid cattle by hiking in national parks, which don't allow grazing except in isolated cases.

Snakes and Other Reptiles

Desert rattlesnakes are fascinating animals, well adapted for life in the harsh environment. Rattlesnakes do not attack people, though they may accidentally crawl in your direction if they're not aware of your presence. Rattlesnakes are more sensitive to ground vibrations than to sound, and ordinarily move quietly away from an approaching large animal such as a hiker. If surprised, they usually coil into a defensive posture and back slowly away. The snake creates its unmistakable buzzing rattle by shaking its tail so fast it blurs. When you hear the rattle, stop immediately and spot the snake before moving carefully away. Never handle or tease any snake.

Bites usually occur on the feet or ankles; ankle-high hiking boots and loose-fitting long pants can stop or reduce the severity of bites. The vast majority of rattlesnake bites are suffered by collectors and people trying to tease or handle a snake. It's very rare for a hiker to be bitten.

The Sonoran coral snake is found only in the deserts of southern Arizona and northwestern Mexico. While extremely venomous, it is reclusive, very small, and would have difficulty biting a human. All other snakes in Arizona are nonvenomous, though they may bite if handled. Rattlesnake bites can be distinguished from bites by nonvenomous snakes by the two puncture wounds left by the venomous fangs, in addition to the regular tooth marks.

The Gila monster possesses a venom similar to that of rattlesnakes but clamps on to its victim and grinds the venom into the wound with its molars. A rare and elusive reptile about a foot long that is protected by state law, the Gila monster is likely to bite only if handled or molested. Don't let its torpid appearance fool you—it can move very fast. Consider yourself very lucky if you even see one.

Develop the desert habit of watching the ground in front of you while moving. Stop before looking around or at distant objects. This habit will save you from encounters with cactus and stepping into rodent burrows, as well as lessen your chance of a surprise confrontation with a rattlesnake.

Snakes prefer surfaces at about 80°F, so during hot weather they prefer the shade of bushes or rock overhangs, and in cool weather will be found sunning themselves on open ground. During the winter cold they are inactive. Any time lizards are active, rattlesnakes probably are active as well.

TIP

Since rattlesnakes can strike no farther than about half their body length, avoid placing your hands and feet in areas you cannot see, and walk several feet away from rock overhangs and shady ledges.

Use a flashlight when moving around camp at dark, at least in the warmer months when snakes are active mainly at night. Never walk around camp barefoot or in sandals during that time of year.

Never kill rattlesnakes found in the wild. They're a vital part of the desert ecology and should be treated with respect, but not feared unnecessarily.

Don't handle a dead rattlesnake; they can strike by reflex for some time after apparent death.

If someone does get bitten by a snake, move safely away from the snake and keep the victim calm. Remove anything on the limb that could become constricting if the area swells. Note the time of the bite as well as the progression of symptoms. If you can, write down the time of the bite and make notes of the symptoms. Seek medical attention as soon as possible. Current medical opinion is that there is no effective first aid treatment. If you are close to a trailhead, hike out with the victim rather than wait hours for rescue. If you are hours from a trailhead, call 911 for a helicopter rescue or use a personal locator beacon. The dangers of infection and tissue damage increase with time.

Arthropods

Venomous arthropods are a much greater hazard in Arizona than rattlesnakes. The small, straw-colored bark scorpion lurks under rocks and logs during the day, and comes out at night to hunt insects. Its sting is life-threatening to children and the elderly. Black widow spiders, identifiable by the red hourglass-shaped mark on the underside, can inflict a dangerous bite. The brown recluse inflicts a bite that may cause extensive tissue damage at the site but is not generally life threatening. These bites seem minor at first but may become very painful after several hours. More painful stings result from the more common but less dangerous scorpions. There is no specific field treatment; young children should be transported to a hospital as soon as possible. The dangerous-looking centipede can produce a painful bite, and also irritate skin with its sharp, clawed feet, but is not life threatening.

Scorpions, spiders, and centipedes can be almost completely avoided by taking a few simple precautions. Avoid placing your hands and feet where you cannot see. Kick over rocks or logs before moving them with your hands. Don't unpack your sleeping bag before you need it in the evening, and always shake out clothing and footwear in the morning before putting them on.

Kissing bugs, also known as conenose bugs, are obnoxious insects that live in rodent nests and feed on mammal blood at night, leaving a large, itchy welt on the victim. They're not a problem during the cooler months, but during the warmer half of the year they give desert backpackers one more reason to sleep in a fully closed net tent.

Ticks are rare in the desert. If ticks are discovered, though, do a careful full-body search every day. It's important to remove embedded ticks before they have a chance to transmit disease, which takes a day or more.

Other insects such as bees, velvet ants, wasps, and the like give painful but nonthreatening stings. The exception is for people who have a known allergic reaction to specific insect stings. Since the reaction can develop rapidly and be life threatening, such people should carry insect sting kits prescribed by their doctors.

A new hazard has recently appeared in the Southwest, the Africanized honeybee. These bees were accidentally introduced into Brazil in the 1960s, and have since spread north to the American southwest. Popularly known as "killer" bees, they have been responsible for about 1,000 human deaths in the Western Hemisphere, and only a few deaths in the United States. In comparison, the common European honeybees cause about one hundred deaths per year in the United States. Although the Africanized bee's venom is no more toxic than the common European honeybees, they are more aggressive in defending their hives and will sometimes swarm on or chase an intruder. The hazard to a person who is allergic to bee stings is obvious. However, every documented fatal case in the Western Hemisphere has involved such an allergic individual, or someone who was infirm or otherwise unable to escape. I have yet to hear of any serious encounter between Africanized bees and hikers.

Avoid all beehives. This includes cultivated bees, which may be a mixture of both types. Cultivated beehives are stacks of white boxes, always found near roads. Wild bees build hives in rock crevices and in holes in trees. Always avoid swarming bees. If attacked, protect your eyes and run away (drop your pack if necessary) and don't swat at the bees. If shelter such as a tent, car, or building is available, use it; otherwise head for heavy brush, which confuses the bees.

There are many scary-looking desert insects that, in reality, are not dangerous. Millipedes, whip scorpions, Jerusalem crickets, sun spiders, and tarantulas are examples of ferocious-looking creatures that are not a threat to humans.

PLANTS

Plant hazards are easily avoided. Never eat any plant, unless you are an expert and know what you're doing.

Some moist areas may have stinging nettles, which as the name implies don't feel good on the skin. Check carefully before sitting or lying on the ground in nettle areas.

Poison ivy grows seasonally along streams and moist drainages in some desert areas. The sap found on the leaves and stems causes a severe skin reaction in many people. It is easily recognized by its shiny, green leaves, which grow in groups of three.

TIP

Avoid touching walking sticks or other items that you suspect may have come in contact with poison ivy. The sap can persist on inanimate objects—and on dogs.

If you accidentally come into contact with poison ivy, or suspect you have, wash the affected skin with water as soon as you can. This will deactivate the sap before the skin has a chance to absorb it.

Calamine lotion can help relieve the itching if you do have a skin reaction.

Cacti

Slow-growing desert plants have developed an interesting array of defenses to protect themselves and their precious moisture from animals, birds, and insects who would like to dine on them. Spines and thorns are some of the obvious features of cacti and cacti-like plants. Most spines are needle-like, and an encounter results in a simple puncture. Warm, southern deserts such as the Sonoran have most of the cacti and thorny plants; the cold northern deserts, such as the Great Basin, have scratchy plants such as sage, and only a few types of cacti.

Teddy bear cholla (sometimes called jumping cholla) looks cute and cuddly. It's not. Each branch is covered with thousands of slender spines, each of which has invisible barbs. If a burr sticks to your skin or clothing, remove it with a pocket comb or a pair of sticks. Then use a good pair of tweezers to pick out the remaining spines. If the spines become deeply embedded, the victim should seek medical attention.

When walking though a cholla field, watch the ground carefully. Most species of chollas have fragile joints that break off easily. The ground around the plants is usually littered with fallen joints, and their spines retain their microscopic barbs until they decay.

Use care around plants with large, spine-tipped leaves such as the agaves and yuccas. The spines can cause deep puncture wounds if you accidentally stumble into them or grab one as a handhold. The edges of the stiff leaves often have hooked thorns that can cause nasty scratches or deeper wounds.

Some small cacti, such as the aptly named pincushion cactus, are small, straw colored, and tend to hide in grass. They are a particular hazard when scrambling up rocky areas.

Catclaw is a bush that sometimes grows in dense thickets. The sharp, curved thorns catch on clothing and skin and have to be carefully peeled off.

Long-sleeved shorts and pants help, but it's best to avoid the thickets altogether.

WEATHER
Heat

During the summer, hot weather is a serious hazard. The lower desert areas may reach temperatures over 120°F, and dehydration, heat exhaustion, and heat-stroke are serious threats. Don't underestimate the consequences of running out of water. As much as 2 gallons of water will be needed by each hiker every day. When temperatures exceed 100°F, a person can survive only a day or two without water.

Even when water is plentiful and the weather moderate, dehydration is still a problem. Thirst is not a reliable indicator of your need for water. Even a slight loss of body fluid decreases your mental and physical abilities, and increases your susceptibility to heat-related medical problems. Always drink more water than required to quench your thirst, and eat snacks to keep your electrolytes up. In very hot weather, it's safer to hike in higher, cooler areas, or to plan hikes that follow streams so water is readily available.

Heat-related illness is difficult to recognize, especially in yourself. By the time the victim is aware of a problem, they are often incapacitated and unable to hike. The first stage, heat exhaustion, is marked by cool, moist skin, goosebumps, heavy sweating, faintness, dizziness, fatigue, a weak, rapid pulse, muscle cramps, nausea, and headache. Treatment consists of stopping and resting in the shade, drinking water or sports drinks.

If left untreated, heat exhaustion can progress into heatstroke (also called sunstroke), which is a life-threatening medical emergency. At this point, the body has lost the ability to regulate its own heat, and only treatment with a hypothermia blanket in a medical facility can save the victim's life. Symptoms include high body temperature, dry, hot, flushed skin, mental confusion, seizures, and coma, nausea and vomiting, rapid breathing, racing pulse, and headache. The victim must be evacuated immediately.

Sports drinks are good because they replace electrolytes as well as water. Snack foods such as nuts and dried fruit also replace electrolytes.

If stranded or low on water in hot weather, conserve your sweat, not your water. Rest in the shade

---

TIP

Always drink the water you have—your body will use it efficiently. Water left in your bottles leads to dehydration.

---

during the day—this reduces your water need by one half or more. Travel during morning and evening, or at night when the air is cooler.

Protection from the heat and the sun is important. Most people find a lightweight, broad-brimmed or desert rat–style sun hat vital for desert hiking. In addition, long-sleeved shirts and pants actually reduce sweating, as compared to bare skin, and also reduce the chance of sunburn and long-term skin damage. Of course, many people find shorts more comfortable. Except in a water emergency, it's a personal choice.

Blisters

Blisters are especially likely when hiking in hot weather. The key is prevention. Wearing two pairs of socks—a thin inner and heavy outer—can reduce friction on your skin and cut down on blisters. Pay special attention to the fit of new boots or shoes, and always take them on a few trial day hikes and shorter backpacking trips before committing to a long trip. Even though lightweight fabric and leather footwear require little break-in, you still want to be certain of the fit.

At the first sign of a hot spot or other discomfort on your feet, stop and have a look. A hot spot can be protected with a piece of felt moleskin. Changing to clean socks will help as well. Once a blister has fully developed, it should be protected by a piece of mole-skin with the center cut out to surround the raised area of skin with padding.

Cold

Snow may fall at any time of year on the higher desert ranges. Be prepared by bringing more warm clothing than you think you will need. During the cooler season, wear synthetic garments made of poly-propylene or polyester fibers. These fibers retain their insulating ability when wet better than any natural fiber, including wool. Avoid continuous exposure to chilling weather, which may subtly lower body temperature and cause sudden collapse from hypothermia, a life-threatening condition. The insidious heat loss caused by cool winds, especially with rain, are the most dangerous. You can completely prevent hypothermia by adjusting your clothing layers to keep yourself comfortably warm, and by eating and drinking regularly so your body produces heat to replace that which is lost.

Like heat exhaustion, hypothermia can be diffi-cult to recognize, especially in one's self. The symp-toms include shivering, slurred speech, slow, shallow breathing, weak pulse, lack of coordination, low energy, mental confusion, and loss of conscious-ness. If hypothermia is allowed to progress to the point where the victim is unable to travel, it is a life-threatening emergency that requires immediate evacuation.

Hypothermia is a hazard in wet canyon bottoms, especially during spring and late fall. If the air is cool as well as the water, you may want to plan the hike for a warmer time of year.

Flash Floods

Heavy rain can occur suddenly in the desert, especially during the late-summer monsoon when thunderstorms are common. Several inches of rain can easily fall in a small area within a few minutes. Because vegetation is sparse, runoff is rapid, and the water gathers force as it collects into the main drainages, the resulting flood often contains as much sand, gravel, rocks, and other debris as it does water, and may travel for miles from the place where the rain fell.

Again, never camp or park a vehicle in a dry wash or drainage. You may never hear or see the storm that causes the wash to flash flood.

If you're in a drainage when water does start to flow, or the existing flow starts to increase, immediately get to higher ground, abandoning equipment if necessary. The main flood can arrive with very little warning.

Flood debris in narrow canyons marks the high
water level.

Never try to cross a flooded drainage or area, either on foot or by vehicle. The water is usually muddy and turbulent, which makes it impossible to gauge its depth. A foot of fast-moving water can easily sweep a vehicle downstream, or knock a hiker down.

Flash floods are especially dangerous in narrow canyons where the high walls prevent an escape. Plan these hikes during periods of stable weather only.

Be aware of the seasonal and long-term weather patterns in your hiking area. If it's a local area, learn the weather patterns in your area, and keep an eye on them before your trip. If you plan to hike in a distant area, check with the land managers for the flash flood hazard.

Get the extended weather forecast from the National Weather Service at the last minute before leaving civilization.

Lightning

Thunderstorms can occur any month of the year in the Southwest, even with snowstorms, but they are most common during late summer. If a thunderstorm threatens, get off high ridges and peaks. Don't camp on ridges or exposed areas during active thunderstorm periods.

If you're caught by lightning, temporarily discard metal objects such as climbing gear or metal walking sticks. Crouch on the ground with your feet close together. Use something insulating such as a sleeping pad between you and the ground, if possible. Don't touch the ground with your hands. Most lightning injuries are not caused directly by the strike but instead by the ground currents that spread out in every direction from the strike. Minimizing your contact with the ground reduces your exposure to the high voltages. For the same reason, don't take shelter under lone trees or in shallow caves.

TIP

Under threat of lightning, spread your party out, so someone will be unaffected by a strike and be able to administer first aid.

Afterword

After this final section on desert hazards, you may be getting the idea that the desert is an unfriendly place to hike. Nothing could be further from the truth. With some knowledge and a few precautions, the desert is an inviting place to explore. After you have some experience, you may find that the desert is as addicting in its own way as the mountains and forests.

Suggested Reading

Clelland, Mike. *Ultralight Backpackin' Tips: 153 Amazing & Inexpensive Tips for Extremely Lightweight Camping.* FalconGuides, 2011.

Fletcher, Colin, and Chip Rawlins. *Complete Walker IV.* Alfred A. Knopf, 2002.

Forgey MD, William W. *Wilderness Medicine: Beyond First Aid.* FalconGuides, 2017.

Grubbs, Bruce. *Basic Illustrated Using GPS.* FalconGuides, 2014.

Grubbs, Bruce. *Exploring With GPS.* Bright Angel Press, 2019.

Jacobson, Cliff. *Basic Illustrated Map and Compass.* FalconGuides, 2008.

Larson, Peggy. *The Deserts of the Southwest: A Sierra Club Naturalists Guide.* Sierra Club Books, 2000.

McGivney, Annette. *Leave No Trace: A Guide to the New Wilderness Etiquette.* Mountaineers Books, 2003.

Roberts, Harry, Russ Schneider, and Ron Levin. *Basic Illustrated Backpacking.* FalconGuides, 2008.

Schneider, Bill, and Russ Schneider. *Backpacking Tips.* FalconGuides, 2005.

Index

About the Author

Bruce Grubbs has a serious problem—he doesn't know what he wants to do when he grows up. Meanwhile, he's done such things as wildland firefighting, running a mountain shop, flying airplanes, shooting photos, and writing books. He's a backcountry skier, climber, figure skater, mountain biker, amateur radio operator, river runner, and sea kayaker—but the thing that really floats his boat is hiking and backpacking. No matter what else he tries, Bruce always come back to hiking, especially long, rough, cross-country trips in places like the Grand Canyon. Some people never learn. But what little he has learned, he's willing to share with you—via his books, of course, but also his websites, blogs, and whatever works. His website is BruceGrubbs.com.